JOBS IN THE COAST GUARD

by Emma Huddleston

Minneapolis, Minnesota

Credits
Cover and title page, © Bruce Leighty/Alamy Stock Photo and © US Coast Guard SCPO NyxoLyno Cangemi/DVIDS; 5T, © Petty Officer 1st Class Seth Johnson/U. S. Deparment of Defense; 5B, © Petty Officer 1st Class Robert S/U. S. Deparment of Defense; 6–7, © Operation 2022 /Alamy Stock Photo, © Petty Officer 1st Class Henry Dunphy/DVIDS ; 8–9, © Chief Petty Officer Sherri Eng/DVIDS; 11, © Chief Warrant Officer Timothy Tamargo/DVIDS; 13T, © Petty Officer 2nd Class Steven Strohmaier/DVIDS; 13B, © Petty Officer 2nd Class Michael De Nyse/DVIDS; 15, © Petty Officer 3rd Class Gregory Harden/DVIDS; 17T, © Petty Officer 2nd Class Etta Smith/DVIDS; 17B, © Petty Officer 2nd Class Etta Smith/DVIDS; 19, © Coast Guard Petty Officer 3rd Class Taylor Bacon/U. S. Deparment of Defense; 21T, © Petty Officer 3rd Class Dustin Williams/DVIDS; 21B, © Coast Guard Seaman Perry Shirzad/U. S. Deparment of Defense; 23, © Petty Officer 2nd Class Dylan Young/DVIDS; 25T, © Petty Officer 1st Class Ayla Hudson/DVIDS; 25B, © Lt. David Connor/DVIDS; 27T, © Operation 2022 /Alamy Stock Photo; 27B, © Chief Petty Officer Alan Haraf/DVIDS; 28T, © Courtesy Graphic/U. S. National Guard; 28B, © Chief Petty Officer NyxoLyno Cangemi/DVIDS; 29, © Seaman Sarah Wilson/DVIDS, © Petty Officer 2nd Class Tara Molle/DVIDS, © Michael Hawkridge/Alamy Stock Photo, and © AB Forces News Collection/Alamy Stock Photo.

Bearport Publishing Company Product Development Team
President: Jen Jenson; Director of Product Development: Spencer Brinker; Managing Editor: Allison Juda; Associate Editor: Naomi Reich; Associate Editor: Tiana Tran; Art Director: Colin O'Dea; Designer: Kim Jones; Designer: Kayla Eggert; Product Development Assistant: Owen Hamlin

Statement on Usage of Generative Artificial Intelligence
Bearport Publishing remains committed to publishing high-quality nonfiction books. Therefore, we restrict the use of generative AI to ensure accuracy of all text and visual components pertaining to a book's subject. See BearportPublishing.com for details.

Library of Congress Cataloging-in-Publication Data

Names: Huddleston, Emma, author.
Title: Jobs in the Coast Guard / by Emma Huddleston.
Description: Minneapolis, Minnesota : Bearport Publishing Company, [2025] | Series: Military careers | Includes bibliographical references and index.
Identifiers: LCCN 2024001597 (print) | LCCN 2024001598 (ebook) | ISBN 9798892320375 (library binding) | ISBN 9798892321709 (ebook)
Subjects: LCSH: United States. Coast Guard--Vocational guidance--Juvenile literature.
Classification: LCC VG53 .H84 2025 (print) | LCC VG53 (ebook) | DDC 363.28/6023--dc23/eng/20240206
LC record available at https://lccn.loc.gov/2024001597
LC ebook record available at https://lccn.loc.gov/2024001598

Copyright © 2025 Bearport Publishing Company. All rights reserved. No part of this publication may be reproduced in whole or in part, stored in any retrieval system, or transmitted in any form or by any means, electronic, mechanical, photocopying, recording, or otherwise, without written permission from the publisher. Bearport Publishing is a division of Chrysalis Education Group.

For more information, write to Bearport Publishing, 5357 Penn Avenue South, Minneapolis, MN 55419.

CONTENTS

Hero in the Sky 4
History of the Coast Guard 6
Beginning a Coast Guard Career 10
Coastie Specialists 14
Help from Above 18
Design Experts 20
Protecting Nature 22
Officers in Charge 24
Beyond the Military 26

More about the Coast Guard 28
Glossary 30
Read More 31
Learn More Online 31
Index 32
About the Author 32

HERO IN THE SKY

A United States Coast Guard helicopter searches through choppy waters below. An aviation survival **technician** on board spots a boater who has gone overboard. The helicopter swoops down closer to the water surface, lowering the aviation survival technician to the boater.

These members of the coast guard are specialty rescue swimmers. They help save people at sea and on land. This important work is just one of the many jobs in the U.S. Coast Guard.

CAREER SPOTLIGHT: Aviation Survival Technician

Job Requirements:
- 22 weeks advanced training
- 24 months service obligation
- Active duty

Skills and Training:
-  Advanced Water Survival
- Emergency Medical Treatment
-  Life Support Equipment Maintenance

Aviation survival technicians sometimes use baskets to carry people to and from a helicopter.

5

HISTORY OF THE COAST GUARD

The United States Coast Guard acted as the nation's first armed forces at sea. In 1790, the U.S. Congress ordered 10 ships to be built to patrol the waters around the young country. Those on board would **enforce** trade laws and work to prevent **smuggling**. The group became known as the Revenue Cutter Service.

Over time, the organization's name and purpose changed. In 1915, it officially became the United States Coast Guard. In addition to enforcing laws, the coast guard was also given duties to help save people from harm at sea. The responsibilities later expanded to include lighthouse operations to help sailors navigate rocky shorelines.

★ ★ ★ ★ ★ ★ ★ ★ ★ ★
Lighthouse keepers maintain the **beacons** on top of lighthouses. These bright lights shine through darkness and stormy weather, signaling to sailors where the coastline is.

A Revenue Cutter Service ship

Guardsmen working on a lighthouse

Today, defense is one of the coast guard's main responsibilities. The members protect the country in different ways during peacetime and wartime. During peacetime, the coast guard sticks mostly to the land and underwater habitats along the coast. They protect **ports**, find drug **traffickers**, and track down **polluters**.

8

During wartime, members of the coast guard work alongside sailors in the United States Navy, helping with search and rescue **missions** or making weather reports for the military. They may be sent to areas all over the world to support those in need.

Members of the U.S. Coast Guard are sometimes called coasties. These coast guard members work hard to protect the country from the waters.

BEGINNING A COAST GUARD CAREER

The first step toward a career in the coast guard is to go through basic training, or boot camp. This intensive 8-week training is made up of physical and mental tests. **Recruits** train to get in shape for their physically demanding jobs. To graduate from boot camp, they must pass a test that involves push-ups, sit-ups, and a 1.5-mile (2.4–km) run. Recruits learn how to use their weapons through target practice. They are also trained in firefighting to handle fire emergencies at sea.

★ ★ ★ ★ ★ ★ ★ ★ ★ ★

Some basic training happens in classrooms, too. Recruits study boating skills and are quizzed on vocabulary for coast guard vessels and equipment.

Coast guard recruits practice carrying heavy ropes used for docking.

After basic training, coast guard members get assigned to roles as either seamen, firemen, or airmen. Seamen are responsible for making sure everything above a ship's deck is working properly. Firemen work with engineers, fixing and maintaining ship parts. Airmen work with pilots on airplanes and helicopters.

While working these first jobs, coasties decide on their more specialized career paths and sign up for additional training. **Enlisted** coast guard members may become officers. These are higher rank members who supervise other coasties. For these roles, enlisted members must attend Officer Training School for 17 weeks.

CAREER SPOTLIGHT: **Seaman**

Job Requirements:
- 17 to 37 years old
- 180 sea service days
- Active duty, enlisted

Skills and Training:
- Deck Maintenance
- Boat Security
- Search and Rescue Aid

Seamen

Firemen

COASTIE SPECIALISTS

Enlisted coast guard members can follow many career paths at sea. Maritime enforcement specialists work on boat stations and cutters, coast guard vessels big enough for crew to live on. They keep the sea safe by catching illegal drug traffickers and polluters. If a person refuses to follow maritime laws, these specialists secure the craft to make sure the vessel and everyone else at sea stays safe. Then, an **inspection** crew checks the ship.

CAREER SPOTLIGHT: Maritime Enforcement Specialist

Job Requirements:
- 10 weeks specialized training
- 24 months service obligation
- Active duty or reserve

Skills and Training:
- Leadership and Communication
- Maritime Law Enforcement
- Tactical Law Enforcement Operations

Maritime enforcement specialists boarding a ship

The many coast guard members at sea often need to communicate with those on land. Operations specialists are the coasties who provide communication between ships and land-based command centers. They work day and night to be available in case of emergencies. Operation specialists respond directly to calls, such as boaters falling overboard. They gather any necessary information for search and rescue missions.

Information systems technicians are technology experts. They keep telephones and computers running smoothly both at sea and on land. This ensures that communication lines between the different parts of the coast guard are always ready.

CAREER SPOTLIGHT: Operations Specialist

Job Requirements:
- 13 weeks specialized training
- 24 months service obligation
- Active duty or reserve

Skills and Training:
- Mission Coordination
- Classified Information Handling
- Operating Navigation and Communication Systems

Information systems technicians are trained to know both computer software and hardware.

17

HELP FROM ABOVE

Once rescue plans are made, response teams spring into action. They help people in dangerous situations, such as those on a sinking ship or people who have been stranded after a hurricane. Two pilots fly the crew into areas that might not be reachable in any way but from the sky. However, pilots can't see what is happening underneath the helicopter. Flight mechanics tell pilots where to go. They also raise and lower gear during the rescue. Rescue swimmers are the ones who dive into the water to save people.

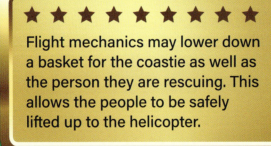

Flight mechanics may lower down a basket for the coastie as well as the person they are rescuing. This allows the people to be safely lifted up to the helicopter.

A flight mechanic searches below

DESIGN EXPERTS

Coast guard engineers help design, build, fix, and maintain advanced machinery and physical structures. Naval engineers are the coast guard experts behind the design and construction of ships and boats. They are also responsible for the operation and maintenance of sea-going vessels, making sure everything is in working order. These engineers make repairs on the ships and boats as needed.

Coasties can also be civil engineers. These specialists are in charge of buildings on land. They plan, build, run, and maintain these structures. Civil engineers make bridges, dams, roads, and water systems.

CAREER SPOTLIGHT: Naval Engineer

Job Requirements:
- 13 weeks specialized training
- 24 months service obligation
- Active duty or reserve

Skills and Training:
- Machinery Operations and Maintenance
- Management and Leadership
- Work Organization and Planning

Civil engineers sometimes use face shields for protection as they work.

PROTECTING NATURE

Those interested in science, biology, and **conservation** can work as marine science technicians in the coast guard. These specialists respond to environmental emergencies, keeping the waters safe and clean. If a ship carrying oil is damaged, leaking oil can kill nearby plants and animals. Marine science technicians help clean up the mess. In addition, they regularly inspect vessels and cargo, paying special attention to the transportation of toxic chemicals. They make sure everything is stored properly. These technicians are trained to safely inspect containers and handle dangerous materials, such as **explosives**.

CAREER SPOTLIGHT: Marine Science Technician

Job Requirements:
- 12 weeks specialized training
- 24 months service obligation
- Active duty or reserve

Skills and Training:
- Environmental Safety Requirements and Regulations
-  Vessel Inspections
- Local Port Security Threat Response

Coasties return a turtle back to the sea

OFFICERS IN CHARGE

Officers in the coast guard supervise enlisted members to keep things running smoothly. Shore prevention officers are experts at preventing accidents. Sometimes, explosives or other dangerous materials are transported by sea. These officers make sure everything goes from one place to another safely.

Sea-going officers lead missions aboard cutters around the world. These officers are responsible for the safety of the crew and for directing navigation. Some are tasked with keeping waterways safe from criminals so that goods can be shipped worldwide.

CAREER SPOTLIGHT: Shore Prevention Officer

Job Requirements:
- 17 to 27 years old
- 17 weeks officer training
- Active duty

Skills and Training:
- Vessel Inspections
- Marine Investigations
- Waterways Management

Sea-going officers use tools to help them navigate.

BEYOND THE MILITARY

The Coast Guard completes important work beyond military missions. It has a whole division dedicated to helping **recreational** boaters. This team is called the Coast Guard Auxiliary. They teach boating safety lessons in the community. This training is meant to reduce injuries and deaths at sea and to protect property.

Whether on military missions or responding to local emergencies, the United States Coast Guard serves its community. Each job plays an important part in communicating, cleaning up, and protecting the sea.

★ ★ ★ ★ ★ ★ ★ ★ ★

Civilians can assist the coast guard by joining the Coast Guard Auxiliary. They volunteer to help enforce laws, patrol coastlines, operate ports, and work on rescue missions.

MORE ABOUT THE COAST GUARD

AT A GLANCE

Founded: August 4, 1790
Membership: More than 55,000 members
Categories of ranks: Seaman recruit, petty officer, chief warrant officer
Largest base: Base Kodiak on Kodiak Island, Alaska

DID YOU KNOW?

★ Douglas Munro is the only guardsman in history to have received a Medal of Honor. He served in World War II (1939–1945).

★ Some dogs work on cutters. They are often called mascots. The animals help coast guardsmen sniff out explosives.

★ The coast guard has three aircraft vehicles called icebreakers. They are used to break through ice.

★ Coast guardsmen attending officer training school are called swabs.

Swabs

GLOSSARY

beacons lights placed high so they can be seen from land and sea, used as a guide or warning

civilians people who are not in the military

conservation the protection of wildlife and natural resources

enforce to make sure a rule is followed

enlisted soldiers who have joined a branch of the armed forces without prior special training and rank below officers

explosives dangerous materials that can catch fire and blow up

inspection a close check of something

missions jobs that have a particular task or goal

polluters people who do not get rid of waste properly

ports coastal cities with docks along waterways where ships can load and unload

recreational done for fun instead of work

recruits people who are going through the process of joining the Coast Guard

smuggling illegally sneaking goods into or out of a place

technician a worker with specialized skills

traffickers people who sell or trade something that is illegal

READ MORE

Conaghan, Bernard. *Coast Guard (Serving With Honor).* New York: Crabtree Publishing, 2023.

London, Martha. *US Coast Guard Equipment and Vehicles (US Military Equipment and Vehicles).* Minneapolis: Kids Core, 2022.

Mason, Jenny. *U.S. Coast Guard (U.S. Armed Forces).* Minneapolis: Kaleidoscope, 2023.

LEARN MORE ONLINE

1. Go to **www.factsurfer.com** or scan the QR code below.
2. Enter "**Coast Guard Jobs**" into the search box.
3. Click on the cover of this book to see a list of websites.

INDEX

auxiliary 26
basic training 10, 12
boat 10, 12, 14, 20, 26
civilian 26
cutter 6, 24, 28
engineer 12, 20–21
enlisted 12, 14, 24
environment 22
helicopter 4–5, 12, 18
information 16–17

laws 6–7, 14, 26
maritime 14
officer 12, 24–25, 28
pilot 12, 18
port 8, 22, 26
rescue 4, 9, 12, 16, 18, 26
safety 8, 14, 22, 24, 26
swimming 4, 18
technician 4–5, 16–17, 22
U.S. Navy 9

ABOUT THE AUTHOR

Emma Huddleston lives with her family in the Twin Cities. She enjoys reading, taking walks, and swing dancing. To all those who serve in the military, she says thank you!